Costa Calida & Murcia
Travel Guide

Quick Trips Series

No part of this publication may be reproduced, stored in a retrieval system, or transmitted, in any form or by any means without the prior written permission of the publisher, nor be otherwise circulated in any form of binding or cover other than that in which it is published and without similar condition being imposed on the subsequent purchaser. If there are any errors or omissions in copyright acknowledgements the publisher will be pleased to insert the appropriate acknowledgement in any subsequent printing of this publication. Although we have taken all reasonable care in researching this book we make no warranty about the accuracy or completeness of its content and disclaim all liability arising from its use.

Copyright © 2016, Astute Press
All Rights Reserved.

Table of Contents

COSTA CALIDA & MURCIA — 5
- Customs & Culture 7
- Geography 8
- Weather & Best Time to Visit 10

SIGHTS & ACTIVITIES: WHAT TO SEE & DO — 13
- Murcia 13
  - Murcia Cathedral 15
  - Murcia Casino 16
  - Museums of Murcia 17
- Cartagena 18
  - Naval Museum 20
- Mazarron 21
  - Roman Salted Fish Factory 23
- Go Wild at Terra Natura 25
- Mar Menor 26
  - Go-Karts Mar Menor 28
- Solaz Boat Trips 29
- Wheels, Walks & Woods 31
- Mud, Mud, Glorious Mud 33
- Águilas Railway Museum 35
- Life on the Ocean Wave 37

BUDGET TIPS — 40

- 🌐 **ACCOMMODATION** 40
  - Pension Balcones Azules 40
  - Pension Segura 41
  - Pensión la Puntica 42
  - Pension Los Cisnes 43
  - Hotel Guillermo 44
- 🌐 **RESTAURANTS, CAFÉS & BARS** 46
  - Murcia City 46
  - Viva Bar & Restaurant 46
  - Juanita Café Bar 47
  - Bar Apicoco 48
  - Restaurante Rierpi 49
- 🌐 **SHOPPING** 50
  - Open-Air Market, Cabo de Palos 50
  - Nuevo Condominia 52
  - Shopping in Murcia City 53
  - Veronica's Market 54
  - Costa Calida Shopping 55

KNOW BEFORE YOU GO   57

- 🌐 **ENTRY REQUIREMENTS** 57
- 🌐 **HEALTH INSURANCE** 57
- 🌐 **TRAVELLING WITH PETS** 58
- 🌐 **AIRPORTS** 59
- 🌐 **AIRLINES** 60
- 🌐 **CURRENCY** 61
- 🌐 **BANKING & ATMS** 61
- 🌐 **CREDIT CARDS** 61
- 🌐 **TOURIST TAXES** 62
- 🌐 **RECLAIMING VAT** 62
- 🌐 **TIPPING POLICY** 63

- 🌐 **Mobile Phones** 64
- 🌐 **Dialling Code** 65
- 🌐 **Emergency Numbers** 65
- 🌐 **Public Holidays** 66
- 🌐 **Time Zone** 66
- 🌐 **Daylight Savings Time** 67
- 🌐 **School Holidays** 67
- 🌐 **Trading Hours** 67
- 🌐 **Driving Laws** 68
- 🌐 **Drinking Laws** 69
- 🌐 **Smoking Laws** 69
- 🌐 **Electricity** 69
- 🌐 **Food & Drink** 70

COSTA CALIDA & MURCIA TRAVEL GUIDE

Costa Calida & Murcia

The Costa Calida on the Spanish Mediterranean coast is a fast growing region with high tourist and residential demand. The region offers historical cities like Murcia (the

COSTA CALIDA & MURCIA TRAVEL GUIDE

capital), Cartagena and Lorca and has interesting local folklore and festivities.

The flat plains stretch along the excellent main road between Lorca and Alicante where you can see far into the distance and where the Revolcadores range of mountains rises to a height of 2,027 metres out of the wide-open landscape.

Far less busy than the better known Costas in Spain, the Costa Calida has much to offer for a relaxing holiday. There are small resorts with quiet beaches to be found and the huge saltwater lagoon at Mar Menor is separated from the Mediterranean Sea by a 30km stretch of sand. Beautiful pink flamingos rest in the Regional Park of Las

COSTA CALIDA & MURCIA TRAVEL GUIDE

Salinas and Arenals de San Pedro del Pintar which are the most important wetlands in the region.

Covering just 2% of Spain's mainland, the region of Murcia is the ninth largest of Spain's autonomous communities and the city of the same name is the main centre for the 45 municipalities contained within it. There are three universities and students from the entire world are attracted to the fantastic learning opportunities and of course the wonderful climate.

🌍 Customs & Culture

The Costa Calida and region of Murcia have an abundance of historical sites and more than enough cultural and architectural experiences to satisfy even the most avid culture vulture.

COSTA CALIDA & MURCIA TRAVEL GUIDE

Surrounded by the beauty of nature there are cave shelters dating back to the Iberian period complete with rock paintings, churches and temples, castles and watch towers as well as military and civil constructions. The history in the region of Murcia has been likened to a rich tapestry that tells a story for our contemplation.

In 825 the Emir of Córdoba, Abderramán II, founded the city of Murcia and it soon grew until it became a capital city. Hundreds of years later the silk industry in the 18th century flourished and brought great wealth to the residents. The evidence of the silk industry can be seen with mulberry trees still lining the streets which once was the staple diet for the silk worms.

COSTA CALIDA & MURCIA TRAVEL GUIDE

One of the most famous landmarks of the region of Murcia is the statue of the Heart of Christ. Situated on top of Monteagudo Castle 4km outside of Murcia city it easily visible for miles and miles around. The statue rises to a height of 14 metres and stands with his arms outstretched in welcome. It is possible to climb the tower but not terribly safe, however plans are in place to build steps and safety rails along with a centre of Argaric culture.

Geography

The Costa Calida covers approximately 250km of Mediterranean coastline from Águilas in the south to Mojon on the Alicante boundary in the north. Named the "warm coast" the 315 days of sunshine each year make sure there is good chance of sunny weather for your stay.

COSTA CALIDA & MURCIA TRAVEL GUIDE

There are a wide variety of attractions here for the visitor including water sports, hiking and archaeological sites to explore plus the largest open area mud baths in Europe and of course long stretches of golden sands with gently lapping waves.

Two airports serve the Costa Calida, the bigger, busier Alicante airport to the north of region and the San Javier / Murcia airport where the runway is right alongside the Mar Menor lagoon. Both airports handle domestic and international flights and have good road access. San Javier / Murcia airport does not have a train station but connections can be made by bus and taxi to Balsicas Mar Menor about 10km away where trains are available.

COSTA CALIDA & MURCIA TRAVEL GUIDE

A Paramount Theme Park has been started not far from Murcia and is due to open in 2015. To meet the expected surge of tourists and their needs for better facilities the nearly completed new airport at Corvera should open sometime before the theme park.

The region of Murcia is accessible by train from many parts of Spain. Murcia Del Carmen train station is just outside of Murcia city for onward transport to the northern end of the region and Cartagena station is a good place for access to the southern end of the Costa Calida and resorts like Mazarron and Aguilas.

🌍 Weather & Best Time to Visit

Temperature differences on the Costa Calida depend on the direction and strength of the winds and the inland and

COSTA CALIDA & MURCIA TRAVEL GUIDE

coastal variations are much more extreme in winter with the coast being at least 4°C warmer most of the time.

The Costa Calida has one of the best climates in Spain and the semi-arid sub tropical climate gives a comfortable average annual temperature of 18 °C. From May to September the temperatures range from 20°C - 27°C and in the winter months from 11°C - 15°C.

In common with the other Spanish areas in summer you will only need a minimum of clothing, light fabrics are best and don't forget your sunglasses, sun cream and a good book.

Spring and autumn can be lovely with days warm enough to go to the beach but be warned, the temperature drops rapidly when the sun goes down so make sure you pack some long sleeves if you are visiting out of the main season.

Of course the natives are wise to this and if you see Spanish children returning to school in September they will already be back into long trousers and jumpers with maybe the odd scarf or two.

Winter can be chilly; many Spanish properties are not geared up for colder weather and tiled floors and no indoor heating means that packing pyjamas, socks and jumpers might be good idea.

COSTA CALIDA & MURCIA TRAVEL GUIDE

Sights & Activities: What to See & Do

🌍 Murcia

www.murciaturistica.es/

Murcia as a city is often overlooked when compared to the more famous names of Madrid, Barcelona and Málaga. To many people travelling through Spain it is just somewhere you pass very close to on a highway as you

COSTA CALIDA & MURCIA TRAVEL GUIDE

whizz past. It is a shame as Murcia has a rich history to offer and many interesting places to see.

For an amazing selection of tapas bars try the Plaza de Flores area in the city centre and Santa Eulalia near the university. The wider main shopping streets have the better known shops but for bargains try some of the local markets.

La Traperia in the centre becomes alive in September for the spectacular Murcia fair with pop concerts, parades, barbeques and bullfight.

At the beginning of Lent a very unusual procession takes place with the Burial of the Sardine. A mock funeral complete with fireworks, floats, dancers and a giant papier-mâché sardine make their way through the streets. Everyone has a wonderful time apart from the sardine that goes up in flames at the end of the day.

Murcia Cathedral

Plaza Cardenal Belluga, s/n

30001

Murcia

+34 968 221 371

When the foundation stone for Murcia cathedral was laid in 1388 by Bishop Pedrosa he probably never realised that the building would take four centuries to complete, a very long period which explains somewhat the widely differing styles of architecture.

COSTA CALIDA & MURCIA TRAVEL GUIDE

Situated in Plaza Belluga the cathedral is the most highly prized historical building in Murcia. There are no less than 23 chapels all with their own artistic designs and magnificent woodcarvings by the Spanish sculptor Francisco Salzillo. With 15th century choir stalls and altarpiece the cathedral is a magnificent building well worth including on your list of things to see.

The West Front of the building with its attractive façade has been acclaimed as an international work of art and is never more beautiful than when viewed at night as the lighting is quite spectacular. Entry to the cathedral is free and opening times are Monday to Sunday 7am to 1pm and 5pm to 8.30pm.

COSTA CALIDA & MURCIA TRAVEL GUIDE

Murcia Casino

Calle de la Trapería, 18

Murcia

+34 968 21 53 99

A must see in Murcia is the casino, built in the mid 1800's. Not actually a gambling house but a Spanish gentlemen's club where for a €1.20 entry fee you can walk through stunning patios inspired by the Alhambra in Granada and see the opulence of long ago eras in the elegant Louis XV ballroom.

For the bargain price of €1 in the ballroom you can dance to the strains of Strauss's Radetzky March while gazing in awe at the 320 light bulbs in the candelabra. The most striking part of the visit is the ladies powder room where the ceiling is dramatically painted and the eyes of the winged woman seem to follow every move you make.

Gigantic windows called La Peceras or fishbowls by the locals flood the two tearooms with light from where you can gaze down on life in CalleTaperia below you. Open from 10.30am to 23.00pm the entry price is just €1.50.

Museums of Murcia

http://www.murciaturistica.es/en/tourism.museums

There are a lot of museums in Murcia covering a wide variety of subjects. Some of them are:

BellasArtes Museum – Fine Arts Collection - www.museosdemurcia.com/mubam/

COSTA CALIDA & MURCIA TRAVEL GUIDE

Archaeological Museum – Archaeology - www.museosdemurcia.com/arqueologicodemurcia/

Bullfighting Museum – History and costumes of bullfighting - http://www.murciaturistica.es/en/tourism.museum?museo=33-2001

Brotherhood of the Most Precious Blood Museum – Sacred Art - www.coloraos.com/

Science and Water Museum – Science and Technology - www.cienciayagua.org/

🌍 Cartagena

Near the southern end of the Costa Calida and located just at the end of the AP- 7 motorway is Cartagena. Established as a major port of call for cruise ships and becoming one of Spain's emerging cultural centres the town was founded around 225 BC.

Home to a large naval shipyard Cartagena is still an important naval seaport and military haven for Spain. Defence was a very important part of Cartagena's history and from the Castillo de Concepción there is an excellent view of the port and city which would have been used as a look out by Carthaginians, Romans, Visigoths, Arabs and Castilians

COSTA CALIDA & MURCIA TRAVEL GUIDE

The main archaeological sites in Cartagena date from Roman times and a key site is a Roman Theatre called Carthago Nova. Five small hills surround the old town in a similar way to the hills around Rome and the influence of the Romans can be seen by a visit to the museum to view the artefacts that have been uncovered in the area.

A music festival held every year in Cartagena brings together around 50 solo artists and groups as they perform on a variety of different stages. The festival lasts for a month and each year the theme is of a different country with the exhibitions and other activities focussing on this country.

A lot of money is being spent on Cartagena to encourage tourists and you can walk along the old harbour and sea walls. Take a seat looking out over the harbour and coastal forts while enjoying a meal or a drink at one of the many bars and restaurants in the area.

Naval Museum

Museo Naval de Cartagena

Antiguo CIM

Muelle de Alfonso XII, s/n

30201

Cartagena

+34 968 127 119

The Naval Museum of Cartagena opened on July 8th 1986 and covers a wide range of sea related topics. Maps of the Mediterranean Sea, the construction of naval vessels in Cartagena, flags and uniforms, naval paintings, submarines and diving are just some of the exhibits and entry is free. The museum is open Monday to Friday from 9am to 2pm.

Mazarron

There are two parts to Mazarron, Puerto de Mazarron on the coast and the town of Mazarron about 3km inland.

Protected by the surrounding bay from the cooler waters of the Atlantic that sometimes creep into this part of the Mediterranean Sea the wide beaches and bays near Puerto de Mazarron are ideal for snorkelling and diving. Divers can visit a popular site called El Arco and go down 35 metres to see a US minesweeper wreck. The water is generally 5°C warmer than the open sea and the climate is pleasant all the year round even in winter.

COSTA CALIDA & MURCIA TRAVEL GUIDE

A 26km long undeveloped beach, the longest in Spain, has undisturbed flora and fauna and whales and dolphins can often be seen playing in the sea just off the coast. The beaches are mostly of coarse grit due to the nature of the surrounding rocks but this doesn't detract from any of the beauty of the coastline.

There are many EU Blue Flag beaches along this part of the coastline so you will be spoilt for choice when looking for that ideal spot to laze away the sunny days. Just be warned, there are some nudist beaches along here so you might spot more than you bargained for.

Take some time to visit Bolnuevo and see the weird sandstone formations. Sculpted by wind and water over

COSTA CALIDA & MURCIA TRAVEL GUIDE

hundreds of years the stones have been weathered into amazing layers and shapes, some balanced so precariously on top of the others that you wonder how they stay up there. For a more energetic few hours take a walk up the cliffs to the highest point at Cabezodel Faro. At the top of the cliff and close to the lighthouse is a figure of Christ with who you can share some of the best views of the town and beaches.

Mazarron town is full of rich history that dates back to Roman as well as Carthaginian times. No matter what time of year you visit you will find fiestas and events taking place that will introduce you to some of the rich colourful Spanish way of life. People in Spain love life and will use any excuse to have a day off work and throw a party.

Roman Salted Fish Factory

La Torre

Edificio Insignia

Mazarron

+34 968 595 242

The Roman Salted Fish Factory is a very interesting and well preserved example of what was a prime product of the time. Discovered in 1976 during construction work the factory was declared of historical interest in 1995 and it is believed that much more of this vast installation is still buried underneath the neighbouring buildings.

During Roman times Mazarron had two important products that were very much in demand throughout the world. These were minerals from the local mines and more importantly, garum, a fish sauce. The process of making garum sauce was long, complicated and extremely smelly, with nothing of the fish being wasted. Rather like olive oil the best quality garum sauce was marketed at high prices with lower grades being sold off cheaply.

Romans were very fond of salted fish and the sauce is thought to have been developed to disguise the taste of food due to preservation, or lack of it, at the time.

Dating from the 4th and 5th centuries many of the large tanks used in the production of the sauce can be seen in the museum. Open hours vary according to the time of year but are generally 10am to 1pm and 5pm to 8pm but it worth checking first before you plan a visit. Entry fee is €2.50 with reductions for children.

Go Wild at Terra Natura

C/ Regidor Cayetano Gago s/n

Espinardo

30100

Murcia

+34 902 505 560

http://www.terranatura.com

The 165,445m2 of Terra Natura wildlife park is home to more than 300 animals of 50 different species, three of these are in grave danger of becoming extinct so extra care is being take to try and preserve them for future generations.

COSTA CALIDA & MURCIA TRAVEL GUIDE

Terra Natura has moved on from the old fashioned way of keeping animals behind bars and now the park has giant window barriers so you feel like you are really in with the animals. There are two themed areas at Terra Natura; the Iberian Peninsula and the African Savannah.

The wildlife park is a wonderful place for a family day out, but children are not compulsory to enjoy the pleasure of a day looking at the varied collection of animals and birds in their natural environments.

Terra Natura opens at 10am each day and closes at 5pm in the winter and 8pm in the summer. Admission prices are €18 for adults and €14 for children.

Mar Menor

A 170km2 saltwater lagoon only separated from the Mediterranean Sea by a 22km long sandbar that ranges from a width of 100 – 1200 metres. The lagoon has a coastal length of 70km and the beautifully warm and clear water never gets deeper than 7 metres.

It has become one of the most popular places in Europe for all kinds of water sports and it has relatively high salinity which aids flotation.

If your preference is to stay above the water with sports like sailing, kayaking and windsurfing then Mar Menor is the place to go.

COSTA CALIDA & MURCIA TRAVEL GUIDE

If your interest takes you further under the water then there are fantastic diving opportunities at Cabo de Palos a few minutes away. There are colourful fish, many shipwrecks and reefs to explore in this protected marine reserve.

The year round ideal weather conditions have made this a very sought after destination for those that want all the advantages of life by the sea but not the frantic pace of the larger resorts.

A long time before the tourists started to arrive here the Moorish kings and Phoenicians chose Mar Menor as the site of their summer residences and with good reason.

Go-Karts Mar Menor

Avenida de Santiago de la Ribera

Dirección Ctra. Stgo. de la Ribera – Aeropuerto

30720

Santiago de la Ribera

Murcia

+34868 10 45 50

http://www.gokartsmarmenor.com/

Go-Karts Mar Menor was opened in 1998 with a track of just 400 metres. By 2009 demand had grown for better facilities and a longer track and the length was increased to 1100 metres with four left hand curves and six right hand curves.

There are different types of karts depending on age and experience. Even small children can enjoy the thrill of racing round the track in the two seater karts accompanied by an adult. For older and more experienced riders there are bigger and faster karts available. With prices from just €8 it is a fun way to see if you are up to taking part in the next Formula One event.

There is a cafeteria where you can refuel yourself ready for your next laps or for non-drivers just sit and watch the rest of the family have some fun speeding round the track.

Solaz Boat Trips

Plaza del Muelle, s/n

Puerto de Mazarrón

+34 606 806 795

COSTA CALIDA & MURCIA TRAVEL GUIDE

www.solazlines.com/

Solaz Lines have two boats and offer a variety of inexpensive boat trips from La Manga and Mazarron. You can choose from trips that stay inside the Mar Menor lagoon or ones that venture out into the open Mediterranean Sea. The boats gently cruise through the still waters with amazing photographic opportunities of the rocky islands and their wildlife.

You can hop on the daily waterbus that goes between the La Manga and Los Alcázares and if you take the trip on a Tuesday the weekly market is just 100 metres away from the quay.

COSTA CALIDA & MURCIA TRAVEL GUIDE

All vessels have full toilet facilities, refreshments are available to purchase on board and there is a dual language commentary. Don't forget your swimming costume and a towel as there is quite often time to stop for a swim in the silky blue water.

There is a full schedule of trips through the summer months and in winter the boats are available for private group hire. The tour prices are from €5 - €13 for adults with discounts for children.

🌐 Wheels, Walks & Woods

Sierra de Espuña

Murcia

+34 968 631 008

http://www.espuna-adventure.com/

COSTA CALIDA & MURCIA TRAVEL GUIDE

When you are fed up with all that sunbathing and inactivity and just don't want to eat and drink anymore, how about working off the calories with some adventure. The regional park of Sierra Espuña is stunning and 25,000 hectares of mainly Carrascoy pine trees offer shade from the blistering Spanish sun.

The forest is odd in that many of the trees are planted in extremely straight lines. In 1889, Ricardo Codorniu, a man with a passion for nature and forests returned to the area to find it decimated of trees due to the prosperity of Murcia and the need for wood. He planted so many trees he became known as the "apostle of trees."

COSTA CALIDA & MURCIA TRAVEL GUIDE

This very well maintained park has hundreds of kilometres of cycling and walking routes with well maintained barbeque and picnic areas. You might just be lucky and see some wild boars or mountain goats with eagles circling overhead as you make your way though this scenic landscape.

The park has a permanent exhibition and visitor centre with information about the flora and fauna in the park and details on walking routes. In the park there are a number of places to see including: Aledo, a peaceful village with an 11th century tower and the Ice Storage Huts, these sunken huts were used during the 16th century to store ice and snow through the summer.

COSTA CALIDA & MURCIA TRAVEL GUIDE

If you want to spend a night or two in the park or visit some of the paths inaccessible to cars why not try quad-biking or 4x4 tours, there are lots of options are open to you, it just depends how brave you are.

🌐 Mud, Mud, Glorious Mud

San Pedro Del Pinatar

Playa de la Mota

Murcia

Have fun and get dirty on your holiday and benefit from the mud baths in San Pedro del Pintar. The climatic conditions in the Mar Menor mean that the mud found in these warm waters has been used for thousands of years for its therapeutic and healing properties.

COSTA CALIDA & MURCIA TRAVEL GUIDE

The rather daunting list of negative and positive ions, chlorine, sulphate, calcium, potassium, magnesium and fluoride sound a pretty scary combination but in fact just the opposite is true. Combined with the extraordinarily fine sand they mix together to make a unique, healing mud. It is highly recommended for arthritis, broken bones, damaged skin and rheumatism as well as a beauty product and you will be carrying on a centuries old tradition.

In the area of Las Charcas at San Pedro Del Pinatar there are specially constructed bathing platforms for those that want to try the healing properties of the Baños de Lodo or Baths of Mud. Just a basic platform with a ladder these simple structures make it easy to climb down into the water and coat yourself with the fine mud. It is like having an all over face pack, plaster the mud all over your body, simply leave it dry and wash it off.

According to local legends you should do this nine times during your holiday for full effect, or as a last result always end with an uneven number of trips. If this seems a bit excessive and the idea of muddy water doesn't appeal there are plenty of more upmarket, and expensive, local spas to visit instead.

A treatment that costs a fortune in the UK can be yours for free, just do a small skin test first with a handful of mud in case of an allergic reaction.

Águilas Railway Museum

Museo del Ferrocarril

Beneath Águilas Railway Station

Paseo de la Estación, s/n

30880

Águilas

+34 667 501 488

When the Águilas friends of the railways and workers association decided to form a railway museum in 1985 where better to put it than in the cellar under the existing railway station.

Strength was the number one watchword back in the 19th century and the main room of the museum was once used as a giant safety deposit box and this is reflected in the very thick walls and enormous iron reinforced door.

In the museum with its vaulted ceilings there are pictures, instruments and objects to tell you all about the history of the Great Southern of Spain Railway or GSSR. There is also a scale model of a working train.

Steam engines used the station at Águilas from 1875 until around 1960 when General Franco created the state railway network and diesel engines took over. A lasting reminder of the popularity of the railways in the town is the locomotive "Águilas" that stands on a plinth in Plaza Isaac Peral close to the harbour.

It is a small museum but worth a visit if you are a train enthusiast or just generally interested in history. Entry is free and the opening hours are 10am to 12pm and 4pm to 6pm with longer hours in the summer.

🌍 Life on the Ocean Wave

Mar Menor

Murcia

+34 616 523 800

www.chartermuffy.com/

Why not pamper yourself and your friends or family and hire a luxury motor yacht or sailboat for the day. If it is adventure you are after try your hand at deep-sea fishing

COSTA CALIDA & MURCIA TRAVEL GUIDE

Within the lagoon of Mar Menor just off the Costa Calida coast there are lots of pretty little islands. La Isla Mayor and Isla delBarón are privately owned but there are several more accessible to the public. All the islands are beautiful and the cruises will take you round the islands of Isla Hormigas with its white lighthouse, La Grossa and El Farallon Reef.

Take a six-hour sailing trip and enjoy the pleasure of being under sail round these beautiful islands. Cool off swimming and snorkelling in the clear blue water off La Grossa from the back of the boat and dine al fresco with a picnic lunch while anchored off shore.

COSTA CALIDA & MURCIA TRAVEL GUIDE

Fishing enthusiasts can go out for the day in search of Barracuda, Merluza, Sea Bream, Red Tuna, Sea Bass and the other fish that are abundant in these waters.

For different night out why not take a short cruise to the Isle of Pediguera and have an evening meal watching the sunset with the twinkling lights of Mar Menor as a backdrop.

COSTA CALIDA & MURCIA TRAVEL GUIDE

Budget Tips

🌐 Accommodation

Pension Balcones Azules

Calle Balcones Azules, 12

Cartagena

30202

Murcia

+34 968 500 042

http://www.pensionbalconesazules.com

Located in the centre of Cartagena, Pension Balcones Azules offers comfortable rooms at sensible prices. All of the 13 rooms have private bathrooms, air conditioning, heating and television.

There is a selection of individual, twin bedded and double rooms available with different grades. Room prices are from €35 for an individual room to €55 for a superior double room.

There is a 24-hour reception, Wi-Fi, fax and a lift. There is a wide choice of places to eat and drink nearby and the proprietors will be happy to recommend somewhere for you.

Pension Segura

Plaza Camachos, 14

30002

Murcia

+34 968 211 281

http://www.pensionsegura.es/

COSTA CALIDA & MURCIA TRAVEL GUIDE

In the heart of the city at the side of the river is Pension Segura. For 40 years Pension Segura has been offering travellers to Murcia a comfortable place to stay in this historic city and it is only 100 metres from the cathedral and places of cultural interest.

The rooms all have private bathrooms, air conditioning and television with Spanish channels and free Wi-Fi. The rooms are priced at €29.50 excluding breakfast or €34.50 with breakfast. The price is per room for one or two guests.

Pensión la Puntica

C/ de Andalucía, 1

San Pedro del Pinatar

COSTA CALIDA & MURCIA TRAVEL GUIDE

30740

Murcia

+34 968 181 034

Only a few steps away from the soft sand of the beach you will find Pensión la Puntica. With a cafeteria and ice cream parlour in the same building you won't have to go too far to find that all important cup of coffee or sit and cool off with one of the many flavours of ice creams on offer.

A mix of single, twin-bedded and double rooms are available, some have room for an extra bed for a third person. A disabled friendly room is also available on request. All the rooms have a private bathroom, air conditioning, refrigerator and television.

Prices are from €25 to €72 for bed and breakfast with other meal plans available.

Pension Los Cisnes

Calle Sierra de Cazorla, s/n

Mazarron

30870

+34 968 153 122

http://www.pensionloscisnes.com/

Only a five-minute walk to the beach and close to the bus station and shops, Los Cisnes offers one, two or three bedded rooms. The rooms all have private bathrooms, TV, heating and air conditioning.

Single rooms start at €20 with a triple room starting at €45, there is an onsite cafeteria and breakfast and meal plans are available.

Hotel Guillermo

Calle Carmen, Nº7

Mazarron

30870

Murcia

+34 968 590 436

The Hotel Guillermo was founded in 1949 by the grandfather of the current director. Since then the family have worked hard to make their hotel a friendly and welcoming meeting place for all to share.

COSTA CALIDA & MURCIA TRAVEL GUIDE

Offering a convenient 24-hour reception and enjoying a central location in Mazarron the Hotel Guillermo is a great place to stay for a night or a few days with plenty going on nearby. Rental bikes are available for hire if you wish to make the most of the beautiful surroundings.

The cafeteria is open for breakfast and offers a wide selection of local foods to try and you can mix with the locals and make friends and try some of the locally produced wines.

There are 16 rooms at the Hotel Guillermo, all have private bathroom, television and air conditioning. Expect to pay €31 per room in low season and up to €56 at the more popular times of year.

🌐 Restaurants, Cafés & Bars

Murcia City

Príncipe de Galés

Calle Vara de Rey, 1,

30001

Murcia

Close to the university and a student favourite is the Príncipe de Galés or Prince of Wales. With buckets of beer containing 12 bottles for €8, and snacks from €1.50 it is very popular and the enormous terrace is always a hive of activity and time of the day or night.

Viva Bar & Restaurant

Avenida España 260

Los Nietos

COSTA CALIDA & MURCIA TRAVEL GUIDE

Cartagena

+34 968 133 111

http://www.vivalosnietos.com

Spread over three levels you can choose to dine in the restaurant, on the terrace or outside on the promenade. Los Nietos has a fantastic seafood menu as well as paellas, delicious steaks aged for 21 days, Galician Lamb cutlets and fresh and colourful salads with a good range of choices for vegetarians. Carefully selected produce is used and prepared with care and there are not just international foods but a whole variety of Spanish dishes are available for you to try.

With a seafront location between Los Urrutias and Los Alcazares and easy access LsNietos is an ideal place for

COSTA CALIDA & MURCIA TRAVEL GUIDE

a meal out on the Costa Calida. If want to leave the car at home the train station is 250 metres from the restaurant.

Juanita Café Bar

Avenida Pedro Lopex Meca

Bolnuevo

Mazarron

30870

Murcia

+34 968 150910

Juanita and her family opened the bar in 1986 and as it is only 100 metres from the beach it is a very popular place to eat. They offer a range of salads, fish, tapas and Murcianspecialities and all the food is homemade on the premises. The à la carte menu is available all the time with the addition of a three course menu for just €8.50 Mondays to Fridays.

Bar Apicoco

Playa Honda

Mar Menor

Murcia

+34 968 563 958

Bar Apicoco is a great family restaurant offering a wide range of familiar foods from home. A summer BBQ replaces the traditional Sunday roast with large selections of meats and a self-serve buffet. The bar has quiz nights, fish and chip specials and even faggots and peas for something completely different.

Restaurante Rierpi

Calle Mayor, 51

Los Belones

Cartagena

30385

Murcia

http://www.restauranterierpi-losbelones.com/

+34 968 137 174

RestauranteRierpe serves simple Spanish food at low prices. They have an excellent range of tapas at lunchtimes and are very popular with locals and expats. Try the guiso de pavo or turkey stew and there are daily set menus and special menus at the weekends.

With seating inside for 250 and outside on the terrace for 60 Rierpi is always busy but you can sit back and absorb the atmosphere of Spanish family life going on around you.

Restaurante Rierpi is open six days a week, closed Mondays.

Shopping

Open-Air Market, Cabo de Palos

Cabo de Palos

Cartagena

Murcia

For those of you who love markets this one will keep you

busy for while. With hundreds of stalls to browse through you might need longer than the opening hours of 8am until 1pm.

Cabo de Palos is a very popular market with tourists looking for a bargain to take home and locals who come to stock up for the week on the freshly picked produce. The stalls are always piled high with goods and if you want to try one of the intriguing fruits or vegetables you don't recognise ask the stallholder for a small sample.

Wander through the myriad of stalls and find some bargains in an amazing display of locally made crafts, clothes and shoes, leather goods and household items.

COSTA CALIDA & MURCIA TRAVEL GUIDE

There are plenty of snack bars selling tapas, snacks, drinks and ice creams, but if you need to rest your weary feet after all that shopping why not have lunch at one of the many fish restaurants in the town.

Make sure you wear sensible shoes as you could be clocking up a few miles round all the stalls. Parking is free and the market is every Sunday.

Nuevo Condominia

Autovía A-7, Km 760

Churra

30110

Murcia

+34 968 701 030

www.ccnuevocondomina.com

COSTA CALIDA & MURCIA TRAVEL GUIDE

With hundreds of shops and restaurants the big new shopping centre just north of Murcia is big enough to keep all the family amused for hours. Easy access off the A7 main road and plenty of parking make it very easy to find all you need under one roof.

With over 20 bars and restaurants there is plenty of choice of where to sit and recover from a hard days shopping, or replenish your energy reserves for another look round just in case you missed anything the first time.

The shops are open from 10am to 10pm Monday to Saturday. The restaurants and cinema open from 12pm to 1.30am Monday to Thursday and 12pm to 3.30am on weekends and holidays.

Shopping in Murcia City

As Murcia is a university town the shopping is at the lower end of the scale rather than designer wear and the prices reflect this.

The are two branches of Spain's biggest department store El Corte Inglés here, but one is very much like another and you could be in any Spanish town when you are inside one of these stores.

Explore instead the tiny, winding back streets and patronise the smaller individual shops. Even if your Spanish vocabulary is limited a friendly smile to the shopkeeper goes a long way in making shopping fun.

In the same area at the heart of the shopping area are Calle de la Traperia and Calle de la Plateria. CallePlateria takes its name from the Spanish world for silver, plata, and here you can still see the silversmiths at work. You can ask to have items of jewelry made for you as a wonderful memento of your visit. Many of the merchants also sell and work with traditional cloths.

Veronica's Market

Calle Verónicas

30004

Murcia,

+34 968 21 51 42

To get a feel for real Spain you need to hunt out the old markets, one of the best ones in Murcia is close to one of

COSTA CALIDA & MURCIA TRAVEL GUIDE

the El Corte Inglés stores. Murcia is not called the vegetable garden of Spain for nothing and the quality of the fruits and vegetables produced here are hard to beat. Named after a long ago and long disappeared convent the market can be found in Plano de San Francisco

Costa Calida Shopping

Shopping on the Costa Calida is very much like shopping anywhere else in Spain. If you keep to the main holiday resorts prices will generally be higher. If you go inland and explore some of the smaller villages you will find local shops that will give you good individual service at often lower prices than the massive chain stores. Just expect to wait a while in the queue while the Spanish ladies chatter on about anything and everything, all far more important than you paying for your shopping.

COSTA CALIDA & MURCIA TRAVEL GUIDE

For stocking up on any forgotten non-food items try one of the Chinese bazaars. A rush of Chinese people moving to Spain has increased the number of these stores throughout the country and some of them are now like giant supermarkets. There are tools and towels, plastic goods and pottery, games and gloves, just about anything you can think of is available in these shops.

Know Before You Go

🌐 Entry Requirements

By virtue of the Schengen agreement, visitors from other countries in the European Union will not need a visa when visiting Spain. Additionally visitors from Switzerland, Norway, Lichtenstein, Iceland, Canada, the United Kingdom, Australia and the USA are also exempt. Independently travelling minors will need to carry written permission from their parents. If visiting from a country where you require a visa to enter Spain, you will also need to state the purpose of your visit and provide proof that you have financial means to support yourself for the duration of your stay. Unless you are an EU national, your passport should be valid for at least 3 months after the end of your stay.

🌐 Health Insurance

Citizens of other EU countries are covered for emergency health care in Spain. UK residents, as well as visitors from Switzerland are covered by the European Health Insurance Card (EHIC), which can be applied for free of charge. Visitors from non-Schengen countries will need to show proof of private health insurance that is valid for the duration of their stay in Spain, as part of their visa application.

🌐 Travelling with Pets

Spain participates in the Pet Travel Scheme (PETS) which allows UK residents to travel with their pets without requiring quarantine upon re-entry. Certain conditions will need to be met. The animal will have to be microchipped and up to date on rabies vaccinations. Additionally, you will need a PETS re-entry certificate issued by a UK vet, an Export Health Certificate (this is required by the Spanish authorities), an official Certificate of Treatment against dangerous parasites such as tapeworm and ticks and an official Declaration that your pet has not left the qualifying countries within this period. Pets from the USA or Canada may be brought in under the conditions of a non-commercial import. For this, your pet will also need to be microchipped (or marked with an identifying tattoo) and up to date on rabies vaccinations.

🌐 Airports

Adolfo Suárez Madrid–Barajas Airport (MAD) is the largest and busiest airport in Spain. It is located about 9km from the financial district of Madrid, the capital. The busiest route is the so-called "Puente Aéreo" or "air bridge", which connects Madrid with Barcelona. The second busiest airport in Spain is **Barcelona–El Prat Airport** (BCN), located about 14km southwest from the center of Barcelona. There are two terminals. The newer Terminal 1 handles the bulk of its traffic, while the older Terminal 2 is used by budget airlines such as EasyJet.

Palma de Mallorca Airport (PMI) is the third largest airport in Spain and one of its busiest in the summer time. It has the capacity of processing 25 million passengers annually. **Gran Canaria Airport** (LPA) handles around 10 million passengers annually and connects travellers with the Canary Islands. **Pablo Ruiz Picasso Malaga Airport** (AGP) provides access to the Costa del Sol. Other southern airports are **Seville Airport** (SVQ), **Jaen Federico Garcia Lorca Airport** (GRX) near Granada, **Jerez de la Frontera Airport**, which connects travellers to Costa del Luz and Cadiz and **Almeria Airport** (LEI).

🌐 Airlines

Iberia is the flag carrying national airline of Spain. Since a merger in 2010 with British Airways, it is part of the International Airlines Group (IAG). Iberia is in partnership with the regional carrier Air Nostrum and Iberia Express, which focusses on medium and short haul routes. Vueling is a low-cost Spanish airline with connections to over 100 destinations. In partnership with MTV, it also provides a seasonal connection to Ibiza. Volotea is a budget airline based in Barcelona, which mainly flies to European destinations. Air Europe, the third largest airline after Iberia and Vueling connects Europe to resorts in the Canaries and the Balearic Islands and also flies to North and South America. Swiftair flies mainly to destinations in Europe, North Africa and the Middle East.

Barcelona-El Prat Airport serves as a primary hub for Iberia Regional. It is also a hub for Vueling. Additionally it functions as a regional hub for Ryanair. Air Europe's primary hubs are at Palma de Mallorca Airport and Madrid Barajas Airport, but other bases are at Barcelona Airport and Tenerife South Airport. Air Nostrum is served by hubs at Barcelona Airport, Madrid Barajas Airport and Valencia Airport. Gran Canaria Airport is the hub for the regional airline, Binter Canarias.

🌍 Currency

Spain's currency is the Euro. It is issued in notes in denominations of €500, €200, €100, €50, €20, €10 and €5. Coins are issued in denominations of €2, €1, 50c, 20c, 10c, 5c, 2c and 1c.

Banking & ATMs

You should have no trouble making withdrawals in Spain if your ATM card is compatible with the MasterCard/Cirrus or Visa/Plus networks. If you want to save money, avoid using the dynamic currency conversion (DCC) system, which promises to charge you in your own currency for the Euros you withdraw. The fine print is that your rate will be less favorable. Whenever possible, opt to conduct your transaction in Euros instead. Do remember to advise your bank or credit card company of your travel plans before leaving.

Credit Cards

Visa and MasterCard will be accepted at most outlets that handle credit cards in Spain, but you may find that your American Express card is not as welcome at all establishments. While shops may still be able to accept transactions with older magnetic strip cards, you will need a PIN enabled card for transactions at automatic vendors such as ticket sellers. Do not be offended when asked to show proof of ID when paying by credit card. It is common practice in Spain and Spaniards are required by law to carry identification on them at all times.

🌐 Tourist Taxes

In the region of Catalonia, which includes Barcelona, a tourist tax of between €0.45 and €2.50 per night is levied for the first seven days of your stay. The amount depends on the standard of the establishment, but includes youth hostels, campgrounds, holiday apartments and cruise ships with a stay that exceeds 12 hours.

🌐 Reclaiming VAT

If you are not from the European Union, you can claim back VAT (or Value Added Tax) paid on your purchases in Spain. The VAT rate in Spain is 18 percent. VAT refunds are made on purchases of €90.15 and over from a single shop. Look for shops displaying Global Blue Tax Free Shopping signage. You will be required to fill in a form at the shop, which must then be stamped at the Customs office at the airport. Customs officers will want to inspect your purchases to make sure that they are sealed and unused. Once this is done, you will be able to claim your refund from the Refund Office at the airport. Alternately, you can mail the form to Global Blue once you get home for a refund on your credit card.

🌐 Tipping policy

In general, Spain does not really have much of a tipping culture and the Spanish are not huge tippers themselves. When in a restaurant, check your bill to see whether a gratuity is already included. If not, the acceptable amount will depend on the size of the meal, the prestige of the restaurant and the time of day. For a quick coffee, you can simply round the amount off. For lunch in a modest establishment, opt for 5 percent or one euro per person. The recommended tip for dinner would be more generous, usually somewhere between 7 and 10 percent. This will depend on the type of establishment.

In hotels, if there is someone to help you with your luggage, a tip of 1 euro should be sufficient. At railway stations and airports, a tip is not really expected. Rounding off the amount of the fare to the nearest euro would be sufficient for a taxi driver. If you recruited a private driver, you may wish to tip that person at the end of your association with him.

🌐 Mobile Phones

Most EU countries, including Spain uses the GSM mobile service. This means that most UK phones and some US and Canadian phones and mobile devices will work in Spain. While you could check with your service provider about coverage before you leave, using your own service in roaming mode will involve additional costs. The alternative is to purchase a Spanish SIM card to use during your stay in Spain.

Spain has four mobile networks. They are Movistar, Vodafone, Orange and Yoiga. Buying a Spanish SIM card is relatively simple and inexpensive. By law, you will be required to show some form of identification such as a passport. A basic SIM card from Vodafone costs €5. There are two tourist packages available for €15, which offers a combination of 1Gb data, together with local and international call time. Alternately, a data only package can also be bought for €15. From Orange, you can get a SIM card for free, with a minimum top-up purchase of €10. A tourist SIM with a combination of data and voice calls can be bought for €15. Movistar offers a start-up deal of €10. At their sub-branches, Tuenti, you can also get a free SIM, but the catch is that you need to choose a package to get it. The start-up cost at Yoiga is €20.

🌐 Dialling Code

The international dialling code for Spain is +34.

COSTA CALIDA & MURCIA TRAVEL GUIDE

🌐 Emergency Numbers

All Emergencies: 112 (no area code required)

Police (municipal): 092

Police (national): 091

Police (tourist police, Madrid): 91 548 85 37

Police (tourist police, Barcelona): 93 290 33 27

Ambulance: 061 or 112

Fire: 080 or 112

Traffic: 900 123 505

Electricity: 900 248 248

Immigration: 900 150 000

MasterCard: 900 958 973

Visa: 900 99 1124

🌐 Public Holidays

1 January: New Year's Day (Año Nuevo)

6 January: Day of the Epiphany/Three Kings Day (Reyes Mago)

March/April: Good Friday

1 May: Labor Day (Día del Trabajo)

15 August: Assumption of Mary (Asunción de la Virgen)

12 October: National Day of Spain/Columbus Day (Fiesta Nacional de España or Día de la Hispanidad)

1 November: All Saints Day (Fiesta de Todos los Santos)

6 December: Spanish Constitution Day (Día de la Constitución)

8 December: Immaculate Conception (La Immaculada)

25 December: Christmas (Navidad)

Easter Monday is celebrated in the Basque region, Castile-La Mancha, Catalonia, La Rioja, Navarra and Valencia. 26 December is celebrated as Saint Stephen's Day in Catalonia and the Balearic Islands.

🌏 Time Zone

Spain falls in the Central European Time Zone. This can be calculated as Greenwich Mean Time/Co-ordinated Universal Time (GMT/UTC) +2; Eastern Standard Time (North America) -6; Pacific Standard Time (North America) -9.

🌏 Daylight Savings Time

Clocks are set forward one hour on the last Sunday in March and set back one hour on the last Sunday in October for Daylight Savings Time.

🌐 School Holidays

Spain's academic year is from mid-September to mid-June. It is divided into three terms with two short breaks of about two weeks around Christmas and Easter.

🌐 Trading Hours

Trading hours in Spain usually run from 9.30am to 1.30pm and from 4.30pm to 8pm, from Mondays to Saturdays. Malls and shopping centers often trade from 10am to 9pm without closing. During the peak holiday seasons, shops could stay open until 10pm. Lunch is usually served between 1pm and 3.30pm while dinner is served from 8.30 to 11pm.

🌐 Driving Laws

The Spanish drive on the right hand side of the road. You will need a driver's licence which is valid in the EC to be able to hire a car in Spain. The legal driving age is 18, but most rental companies will require you to be at least 21 to be able to rent a car. You will need to carry your insurance documentation and rental contract with you at all times, when driving. The speed limit in Spain is 120km per hour on motorways, 100km per hour on dual carriageways and 90km per hour on single carriageways. Bear in mind that it is illegal to drive in Spain wearing sandals or flip-flops.

You may drive a non-Spanish vehicle in Spain provided that it is considered roadworthy in the country where it is registered. As a UK resident, you will be able to drive a vehicle registered in the UK in Spain for up to six months, provided that your liabilities as a UK motorist, such as MOT, road tax and insurance are up to date for the entire period of your stay. The legal limit in Spain is 0.05, but for new drivers who have had their licence for less than two years, it is 0.03.

Drinking Laws

In Spain, the minimum drinking age is 18. Drinking in public places is forbidden and can be punished with a spot fine. In areas where binge drinking can be a problem, alcohol trading hours are often limited.

Smoking Laws

In the beginning of 2006, Spain implemented a policy banning smoking from all public and private work places. This includes schools, libraries, museums, stadiums, hospitals, cinemas, theatres and shopping centers as well as public transport. From 2011, smoking was also banned in restaurants and bars, although designated smoking areas can be created provided they are enclosed and well ventilated. Additionally tobacco products may only be sold from tobacconists and bars and restaurants where smoking is permitted. Smoking near children's parks, schools or health centers carries a €600 fine.

🌐 Electricity

Electricity: 220 volts

Frequency: 50 Hz

Your electrical appliances from the UK and Ireland should be able to function sufficiently in Spain, but since Spain uses 2 pin sockets, you will need a C/F adapter to convert the plug from 3 to 2-pins. The voltage and frequency is compatible with UK appliances. If travelling from the USA, you will need a converter or step-down transformer to convert your appliances to 110 volts. The latest models of many laptops, camcorders, cell phones and digital cameras are dual-voltage with a built in converter.

🌐 Food & Drink

Spanish cuisine is heavily influenced by a Moorish past. Staple dishes include the rice dish, Paella, Jamon Serrano (or Spanish ham), Gazpacho (cold tomato-based vegetable soup), roast suckling pig, chorizo (spicy sausage) and the Spanish omelette. Tapas (hot or cold snacks) are served with drinks in Spanish bars.

The most quintessentially Spanish drink is sangria, but a popular alternative with the locals is tinto de verano, or summer wine, a mix of red wine and lemonade. Vino Tinto or red wine compliments most meal choices. The preferred red grape type is Tempranillo, for which the regions of Roija and Ribera del Duero are famous. A well-known sparkling wine, Cava, is grown in Catalonia. Do try the Rebujito, a Seville style mix of sherry, sparkling water and mint. The most popular local beers are Cruzcampo, Alhambra and Estrello Damm. Coffee is also popular with Spaniards, who prefer Café con leche (espresso with milk).

Websites

http://www.idealspain.com

A detailed resource that includes legal information for anyone planning a longer stay or residency in Spain.

http://spainattractions.es/

http://www.tourspain.org/

http://spainguides.com/

http://www.travelinginspain.com/

http://wikitravel.org/en/Spain

COSTA CALIDA & MURCIA TRAVEL GUIDE

Printed in Great Britain
by Amazon